Ope'

Collected Poems

Yulu Ewis

Introduction by Carolyn M. Dunn

Winner 2018: First Book Award for Poetry,
Native Writers' Circle of the Americas (NWCA)

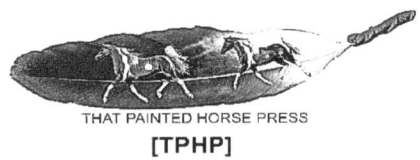

Harrah, Oklahoma
Calgary, Alberta
2021

Ope'

© Yulu Ewis/Kristen Debler

ISBN 978-1-928708-06-3

Except for use in fair use or reviews and/or scholarly considerations, no part of this book may be reproduced, performed, recorded, or otherwise transmitted without the written consent of the author and permission of the publisher.

Introduction by Carolyn M. Dunn © 2021

Cover Art: Tiffany Adams © 2020

Author Photo: Kristen Debler © 2020

Editor: Carolyn M. Dunn with RPC
Book Design: That Painted Horse Press RPC
Layout Editor: Marley Roppolo
Editorial Assistant: Noémie Foley
Cover Design: TPHP RPC

That Painted Horse Press: A Borderless Indigenous/BIPOC Press of the Americas
https://thatpaintedhorsepress.blogspot.com

Dedication

People come and go in our lives, but those who leave footprints on our souls inspire us to become the best part of ourselves. The people that have left footprints on my soul are worth mentioning. I would like to dedicate these words to:

My Parents, Kimberly Sharp and Scott Debler. Thank you for letting me memorize my stories to read to you at bedtime.

Kim Spottiswood. Thank you for teaching me that reading could be fun. I will always remember, "Halfway down the stairs is a stair where I sit. There isn't any other stair quite like it." A.A. Milne

Julie Motes, now Julie Uren (7th and 8th grade English teacher). Your dedication in having me create my first fountain poem opened up my eyes to the world of poetry.

My Grandparents, Lawrence Debler and Edsella Mae Debler. Thank you for singing with me in the car, for making me grilled cheese and watching cartoons with me and mostly – for teaching me about family, my culture and my ancestors. You are missed but never forgotten.

To Grandpa and Grandma Wilbur and my Great Grandma Genny. Thank you for providing me with a great place to grow up and to be myself and for teaching me the true meaning of family.

To my siblings Brandon Debler and my Melanie Buelna. Thank you for showing me unconditional love and support.

Kristian Smith. Your outlook on life inspires me.

Cheyenne Marie Quitanilla. Thank you for always putting a smile on Gaga's face.

Jace Carr. Thank you for teaching me how to be your Gaga.

Jessica Scott. Thank you for being the encouraging voice in my ear all these years

Mary Anne Fassel. Thank you for being my rock in a world full of pebbles.

Rebecca Robles. Thank you for believing in me and teaching me how to fight for the land.

Uncle Jimi Castillo. Thank you for dancing for me and teaching me about the world of spirits and ancestors.

Kimberly Neketin. Thank you for being by my side when I was trying to find my voice

Contents

Introduction..i
Helanye 2
Basket Hymn 3
'Oye's Confession..5
Pollopaksy..8
Red Heart and Invisible Dreams..............10
Powerless Honor (Memoirs of a Tribal Nation......12
Angry Basket...15
Blind Faith................................,..............18
Dream-Weaver..19
Tollepa<u>ti</u> 21
Prison of Heartbreak I..............................22
Prison of Heartbreak II.............................23
Hawu<u>s</u> na 24
Ka Yomu 25
Changing Wind 27
Tow<u>is</u> Hinak 28
We Are Manik...29
Paint it Blue..30
Honor's Song..31
'Oye Speaks...32
Ma Tala<u>s</u>..35
Afterword: Voice of the Silenced.............39
Glossary...46
About the author......................................48

Introduction: Words Made of Beargrass: Truth-telling the Ancestors

I was born in Southern California to parents who were both born in California. Their parents came from the "old country": Louisiana, Mississippi, and Oklahoma in the 1930's in search of ways to start over again, after the federal government had destroyed their tribal nations and cultures in order to rid tribal peoples of their languages, cultures, religions and lifeways. We were diasporic Indigenous peoples, leaving one homeland that never really belonged to us, one we were forced out of and into a new one; and one that was woven from the sea salt grasses along the Louisiana prairie from three distinct strands to become one. Though I consider myself a Californian, and I am an Indigenous person, I've long said that I'm not a California Indian *but* I am an Indian from California. There's a difference between the two. In this first volume of poetry from Coastal Miwok/Lower Pomo writer Yulu Ewis, the poet situates her voice within the interwoven history, memory, and orality of her tribes, giving the reader fresh insight into the history of the California Indian world.

While the federal government legislated dispossession of Native nations in the south, long after defining "Indian Country" through the Indian Commerce Clause, forcing Indians to cede any and all land to the federal government only, California was slowly shedding Mexico and leaning toward inclusion in the United States, cementing American control from the Atlantic to the Pacific. The narrative of California shifted, moving from Indian control to Spanish colonialism, then to Mexican and then to American. Settler colonial shifts were devastating to California Indians. While the Spanish succeeded in colonizing Indians through forced labor and forced religion, the Mexican Californios enslaved through their rancherias, and soon Americans outright murdered Indians. John Rollin Ridge, Cherokee writer and diasporic Indian, relocated to California from Indian Territory to escape murder charges, brought against him for avenging the bloody murder of his father, John Ridge. An educated journalist, Rollin Ridge took up for California Indians, despite his own belief in the intellectual superiority of the Cherokee over other American Indians. In telling his own story of Cherokee dispossession, removal, and his father's complicity in these actions, he used the story of a California Indian Mestizo (*The Life and Times of Joaquin Murrieta, California Bandit*) railing against the colonization of California Indians as a metaphor for his own life story.

    While the southeastern nations were (and still are) creating a new world in the aftermath of forced relocation from our ancestral homelands, California Indians were recovering from the mission colonial period, about to enter into the gold rush that saw legislation in the state of California that paid top American dollars for California Indian scalps. Legalized murder of California Indians, long dehumanized by both the Spanish and the Americas, was widely genocidally practiced. Southern and Central coastal California's missions had been abandoned by the Spanish in favor of the Mexican ranches that enslaved California Indians into indentured servitude, and often sent hundreds if not thousands of Indians off land in the Pacific slave trade. California Indians were facing a new genocide that had divide and conquer written all over it. Often scattered due to missionization, the need for work and the loss of lifeways, California Indian families were often separated, geographically, culturally, and linguistically. Many had adopted Spanish names, cementing their Mestizo status as mixed race, not as Indian. Their histories became merged with the histories of the Mexican rancheros, and the American colonizers, that gave rise to the narrative of the "vanishing Indian" in California. The histories of many so-called "Mission Indians" were relegated to the distant past, or forgotten completely as California lurched toward statehood and beyond. This book, the first by California Indian poet Yulu Ewis, restores that narrative that California Indians survived, and that they can - and do thrive, despite the hurdles they still face. This is, in many ways, history told through poetry, and poetry as history.

Yulu Ewis tells us that storytelling in California Indian cultures, specifically in her Coastal Miwok/Southern Pomo identity, that stories connect us in language to landscape to history. "Traditionally," she writes in the afterward of this book, "oral histories or stories told by our elders were our voices; they were the very essence of our cultural identities." Her tribes were relocated early in the twentieth century as "landless Indians" in Sonoma County, just north of San Francisco by seventy-five miles. In 1958, the federal government terminated its relationship with this group and they were left, like so many California Indians, to fend for themselves in a place where they had long been viewed as outsiders by the colonial majority. Organizing as the Federated Indians of Graton Rancheria in the early 1990's, they would later have their recognition restored by President Clinton in 2000. This long road to recovery is similar to many California Indians fighting to have their sovereignty restored; but this story is not just about sovereignty. It is the story of a people who have always known who they were, who they are; and their stories and songs and language remain in the narratives they have told over and over again since time immemorial.

In this first collection of her work, Yulu Ewis tells us of those dark times in tribal history: going from Indian, to Spanish, then to Mexican, and lastly to American control over a three hundred year period. Her poem, "Basket Hymn," anchors this collection in that history that was lost, but never to the Miwoks and Pomos who lived it:

> "Blessed Be Your Name in purified lashes from the whip upon my brother's back. Blessed Be Your Name in the collection of our hair. Blessed Be Your Name in the stripping of our honor. Blessed Be Your Name in Stealing our Power! Blessed Be Your Name in the tithe you collect to kidnap our children."

Stories of colonization are woven in the beargrass of her ancestors, falling to the page in ripples that will affect generations who come to know the power of the story of this sovereign nation, and of many sovereign nations in California, recognized or not. The beargrass words are woven so tightly that the Miwok language, Spanish, and English, along with the Catholic faith forced upon the ancestors, roll into one, creating this modern nation inflicted with truth telling and now with the power to tell their own stories. The power to tell has always remained, and the voice of this poet is here to weave these stories into the light of this world.

~Carolyn Dunn
Oklahoma City, Oklahoma, 2020

Ope'

Collected Poems

Helanye

Idol Moon cooks from cold
Shock, *Kayaaki* looks to drown
Sorrows; borrow
comforts from poor lost fools.

Basket Hymn

In the land that is plentiful, which he has created in love Blessed Be Your Name
Anointed Sing Hosanna to the Highest Praise to Adonai the Father Blessed Be Your Name.
In the house of the Rock Blessed Be Your Name. In the Missions of Junipero Serra Blessed Be your Name! In the *kochcha* of the Neophyte Blessed Be His Glorious Name.
Blessed Be Your Name in Murder! Blessed Be Your Name in Bondage!!
Blessed Be Your Name in *Espanol*. Blessed Be Your Name in '*Olom*.
Blessed Be Your Name When he sells his soul in the baptismal fount. Blessed Be Your Name!
Blessed Be Your Glorious Name.
Blessed Be Your Name '*Oye* in pain. Blessed Be Your Name '*Ay kooya* in Shame.
Blessed Be Blessed Be Blessed Be in sickness infested blankets! Blessed be Your Name '*Unu* in sacrifice. Blessed Be Your Name in the redness that feeds the waters. Blessed Be Your Name in hand stained red victory. Blessed Be Your Name in mass unsacred burials of our ancestors.
Blessed Be Your Name in purified lashes from the whip upon my brother's back. Blessed Be Your Name in the collection of our hair. Blessed Be Your Name in the stripping of our honor. Blessed Be Your Name in Stealing our Power! Blessed Be Your Name in the tithe you collect to kidnap our children.
Blessed Be Your Glorious Name in the confessional killing of our traditions. Blessed be Your Name in the Desecration of our Song! Blessed Be Your Name in the Death of our Spirit! Blessed Be Your Glorious Name.
Blessed Be Your Name in the one who leads our tortured souls to Heaven. Blessed Be Your Name in the tainted saint who in the end meets us there.

Blessed Be Your Name Burning in Glorious Red Fire. Blessed Be Blessed Be Your Glorious Name. Delivering us as an offering to Praise You.

'Oye's Confession

'Oye shivered.
The wind
Bit goosebumps into his arms,
He cradled himself,
Embracing the nothingness.

A feather flew by
And yanked his nose hairs.
He sneezed.
"AAAACHHOOOOO!"

He threw the feather into the air.

"That's not how you do it."
The Priest said,
Rubbing the rosary beads between his fingers.
"Your power's no good here anymore."

'Oye, chewed on a piece of tree bark,
Spit on the ground
And watched it nourish the mother
Flowing in her like water,
The essence of life.

The priest chuckled
Kissing the tree that hung from his neck.
Dumping a vial, he pulled from his pocket
Dumping a vial, blessed in the name of the Father
Dumping a vial, blessed in the name of the Son
Dumping a vial, blessed in the name of the Holy Spirit,
Of water that washed death over his children.

'Oye's feet
Stomped on the soft ground below him,
Hearing her heartbeat,

He danced.

Stomp.
Dance.
Let it Rain.

Stomp.
Dance.
Let it Rain.

Let the movement of my heart,
Bless you,
Bless you.

Let the movement of my heart,
Cleanse you.

A spark, hidden in the buckeye tree,
Darted and ran
To kiss the sagebrush.
Purifying the air around them.

The Priest coughed
Clear puffs of smoke
Rinsed the venom from his lungs.

"My God is greater than you." He said,
Singing a dry hymn of praise
Falling on deaf ears and drowning souls.

'*Oye* eyed the Priest,
The man who challenged his power.

'*Oye* opened his mouth,
turned his head,
swished his tail,
 And blew.

He knew words held great power.
He knew there was wisdom in silence.

He jumped on a moonbeam
Rode it to the sky,
And waited,
For '*ay kooya* to call him home.

Pollopaksy

The star dust child's head ducks below the blanket,
eyes tightly shut,
hiding from 'Axeki,

She sings a lullaby,
Her shadows dance,
On the walls of his eyelids.

He prays.
The monsters of the night come alive.

'Oye laughs.
He runs by, leaving
the child fends for himself.

'Axeki, caresses the child's hair.
He shivers.
She lures him
Into her nightmares.

The star child becomes stuck.
Grandmother Dreamweaver has been fishing tonight,
She has caught him in her clutches, and
He struggles.
Spider Woman dangles,
Starring in the child's face.

He screams.
She grabs him.

She drools, teeth exposed
Staring at her bountiful feast.

Squeezing his eyes tight,
Her mouth opens wider.

Dawn appears, and the shadows
Swim towards the edge of the world.

Father Sun and his rays
 Pick up their drums, ascending towards morning

The star dust child's eyelids start to flutter,
Erasing the dreams attacking him in the night.

Sage tickles his nose, purifying the room.
The star child cleans

Red Heart and Invisible Dreams

i.

Grandmother Spider
Weave the web.

Star dust children
 Unfold the blanket of night.

Mother Half Moon
Light the way.

Honored ancestor
Pick up the drum, and play.

We are waiting to dance.
We are ready to dream.

ii.

Wake me up!
I'm dreaming.

Dare I dream?

The blanket of stars surround me
Singing a lullaby to my conscience
About a world that will never be,
 Especially for me.

Star dust wakes me,
Mocking, squawking,

Disguised as Coyote,
His drums start beating,

Images fly,
Prophecies reveal, and
Wisdom unravels
a memory,

The arrow pierces hope,
Scalping its innocence,

Leaving the blind dream to its fate;
Invisible, peaceful,
Slowly kills its victims,
Catching their sacrificed hearts,
Within its web.

Grandfather, patiently works his primal dreams
Coddling them;
Giving them courage,
Teaching them honor.

His dreams resemble hope,
His dreams resemble survival.

Do we dare to reveal them?
Let them go!

Powerless Honor (Memoirs of a Tribal Nation)

"Oh Ancestors, sing the song of war,
Of honor to the warriors who continue to fight
The never-ending battle,
Their never-ending battle for peace!"

Dance.
Hena Mi.
Move your feet,
For the love of a nation.

"Wake up," Coyote says as he laughs at our newfound civil liberties of 1968, *"Love is dead."*
Throwing the Bill of Rights in our face,
"Written in a language that seals our fates,"

Dance...
To honor the death of a people
Hena Mi...
To the dictation of sovereignty
Move your feet and praise
The limiting of our government
For the selfishness of another nation;

"Ka machchaw," the elders say.
And become invisible.
"Submit" and we'll be saved.
Stop dreaming.
Stop being who we are,
And we'll be left alone

Howchia calls us to listen,
to the story of an invisible people.
Listen! Do you hear their voices?
The voices of the distant ancestors?
Listen closely; it's hard to hear the whispering wind.

But, if you are patient enough you can hear the beat
As it whisks by, in one ear and out the other.

Hear me. They say.
Who are these people? They ask.
They are unfamiliar, quiet in their distress.
Speaking in a language we do not understand.,
existence limited to the reservation,
honor living on through the stereotypes of tomahawks, scalping, and war woops.
dances honor assimilation, genocide and
Economic dependency (through the welfare system and Tribal Casinos),
There is no other way for economic independence.

What happened to the education of our peoples?
We carry it with us.
What happened to our pride?
We carry it in us.
What happened to our voices?
We carry them within us.
What happened to our leaders?
We carry their blood inside us.

"What are we to do now?" They cry out.
Do we hear them?

Are we lost within our own greed?
We will continue to fight.
Have we forgotten who we are?
We will continue to thrive.
Have we lost our voices?
We will continue to sing.

I will find my voice.
I will fight for a better tomorrow?
I will be heard.

I hear the wind as it goes by....
She tells me to listen,
To be patient.
In her language
She speaks to my blood.

Angry Basket

Dedication: To honor all of the people who are fighting to keep the old ways; those who have suffered disenrollment. I pray that we can work together and save our people from this plague called greed.

i.

'Oye stands watch;
He listens to the chant of the people.
He rejoices as their voices rise up
As they gather in solidarity.

"We are the '*Olomko*
The Mighty, Mighty '*Olomko*.
Fighting for our Motherland.
Fighting for our honor."

'Oye dances
To the beat of their steps.
He prays -
their words reach the stars.

He weeps -

ii.

Grandmother Dreamweaver picks willow to weave together an age-old tradition
Binding the fabric of our hearts.
Dipping the branches in water she tests their resistance,
Strengthening the knot,
A movement that has been repeated for generations

'Oye stood on the top of *Tamal Payis*
He stared in awe
At the power of her work;
The creator of dreams; a vessel that safely holds the songs of the people,

Medicine to protect them from harm.

Angry Basket was born
The honor of the' *Olomko*
The joy of the land
The soul of the ancestors.

Kule picked her up and nuzzled her like one of her cubs.
She threw her on her back
And danced to the conjoining pulse of all creation.

iii.

Angry Basket grew up
The honor of the '*Olomko*
The joy of the land
The soul of the ancestors.

Angry Basket's hair flowed
To the bottom of her feet
Angry Basket's hair
Was the pride of the *Huukuyko*

Angry Basket's hair flowed in the wind
Its reflection
Her shadow in the fire,
Delighted and thrilled her.

Angry Basket took pride in the story of her making
Her name on the tips of tongues
Made her ears prick,
Feeding the hunger in her belly,
making her hips sway.

The strengthening bond between the people and
Angry Basket started to unravel,
Like the sealing thread in an age old quilt.

Angry Basket no longer listened
Angry Basket no longer danced
Angry Basket no longer loved.
Angry Basket only respected power
Angry Basket only respected herself.

Angry Basket was born
The honor of the '*Olomko*
The joy of the land
The soul of the ancestors.

Angry Basket became
The plague of the '*Olomko*
The tears of the land
The death of the ancestors,
The thread that bound a Nation.

Blind Faith

Scary, what can bring you to your knees.
The taste bursts
Like a bite from a berry
Settling in the pit of your stomach
Gnawing hunger
A thirst, yearning for
A need you can't explain.
Your soul divided
Someone callin' your name
Confusion surrounds you
Pulls you
Until you feel it tingling throughout your body.
Your body yearns for peace
Your mind is spinning out of control
Unraveling the very essence of your consciousness
Pulling apart the reeds that built a basket.
You feel broken and unyielding
Somethins' gotta' give!
Screaming in your face
Back against the wall
dripping, stretching
Your body twisting
Into compliance,
humbly crawling into the unknown.

Dream-Weaver

Dream-Weaver Grandmother sits by her loom,
Spinning her creation as intricately as Spider Woman,
Each finger weaving the fabric of a
Story, prophecy, and even a nightmare

Grandmother hums a lullaby
As my body's laid to rest,
Head to pillow,
Eyes closed shut
She sets the stage for our nightly journey.

She runs her hand over her loom,
Opening the door,
Allowing my mind to walk into the light of night.

Grandmother, your world is full of beauty and light.
Why is there fear running through my veins?
A smile appears on her face,
Holding her hand in mine,
She squeezes it in reassurance.
'*Ay kooya*, the road of the known and the un-known are one and the same,
This is a gift I share with you,
Use it wisely,
She says as she tightens the strings on her loom.

A picture comes into view,
Images rushing, dancing in my mind's eye,
The stories and the prophecies went through
The nightmares stuck into the folds of the web.

I squeeze her hand harder,
Her presence soothes me.

Grandmother, I am scared of what you

Prophesy to me,
What you allow me to see.

Will my ancestors weep for me?
Will I see my people extinct?
A meaning I can't even fathom...
No longer hear my native tongue, giving me
This story?

A lullaby rises from her lips,
Quieting the fear within my soul.
'*Ache, come* to life,
wake the warrior
Born within you.

Be strong,
Prepare for death,
String the arrow
shoot the enemy you have allowed in.

The night light bounces off the eclipse,
Encompassing the world in its shadow.
Grandmother gently tightens the strings,
Marveling at her creation;
Grandmother, please don't let this nightmare seep through
your protective web,
tie this thing up and suck its life.

Will you let the Ancestors speak to us?
Yes.
Will you let our dreams seep through your web and live?
Of course, 'Ay kooya.
Will you bind these words to my heart?
Yes, *'Ay kooya.* Bound so I may remember them?
Yes, Akooya.
And now you shall wake!

Tollepati

Coyote puckers his lips
Gracing her with a sweet kiss.
He catches her face in a loving embrace; brace
Yourself for the scent of a trick – in disguise.

Prison of Heartbreak I

I surrender to the noise within my head.
I tried to fight it with every fabric of my being.
The voice inside leaves me with dread,
to the point where I no longer know what I am seeing.
The voice in my head sang to me,
the beat beckoned my soul,
allowing it to move and to be free;
testing the limits of my self-control.
The song led me to a spiritual revival;
joyous at my new found liberation.
Blessed from a book that did not come out of The Bible,
something that led to my soul's humble separation.
Freeing me from my own personal bondage was a rewarding task.
Keeping me alive another day is all that I ask.

Prison of Heartbreak II

The black shadow on the wall forces itself inside my head
A drumbeat of darkness moves within my being.
The voice of *'Axeki*, the spirit monster, leaves me with dread,
As bars slam in my face and limit the world I am no longer seeing.
Her voice comforts and sings to me,
Her lullaby becomes my constant companion, it beckons my soul,
Ironically allowing it to move and to be free
Testing the limits of my torture; pushing the boundaries of my self-control.
Her lullaby awoke within me, a spiritual revival;
Breaking out; joyous at my new found liberation.
Finally blessed, *Walking the Red road*, a book that did not come out of the Bible,
Something that led to my soul's humble separation.
Freeing me from my own personal bondage was a rewarding task.
Keeping me alive and away from *'Axeki* is all that I ask.

Hawus na

Kayaaki's sweet breath
opened the world.
Feathers flew and became life.

Ka Yomu

Every space
Every matter in the world contains a beat
A spark of something alive
A sense of something special and unique

Water is renewed by the rain
Sunshine is given by the sun
Air is given by the trees
Plants are formed by the nutrients in the ground,
The Earth is alive under your feet

They are the songs sung within our hearts
The words flowing within our veins
Beating a rhythm of genuine connection
Reminding us of our responsibility
Reminding us of our voices

They sing about peace and harmony
They sing about love and companionship
They sing about the importance of giving
 They sing about leaving something behind for the next generation

They tell you that it's not about creating a name for yourself
They say a name can be changed like the direction of the wind
Thrown out or discarded like trash in a bin.
They tell you that it's about being a leader,
When the time calls
It's about being a follower,
When a good path has been formed.

It's about the struggle and where it brought you.
It's about being hopeful and what that makes you
It's about being honest and how that frees you
It's about being truthful and how it can redeem you.

Names can be said in many different ways
How can they hold us down and define us?
Colors can be painted in many different hues
How can they hold us down and define us?
Money can be earned in many different ways
How can it hold us down and control us?

A beat is laid in each and every one of us
Thump, thump
Thump, thump
It is our connection to each other
It is the universal sound that we should follow

Changing Wind

A searching wind blows into the night and stirs the dancing embers of the fire. Little star children are fighting profusely; back and forth. Little scenes of twinkle dust dancing, bouncing, painting shining images in the sky for the world below. Who is to wake up Mother Half Moon and tell her the news? That finally the wind is changing. Blowing in her direction. Giving her the chance to fully grow again. Coyote stops dancing with the Star Woman. Covered in star dust he leaves her and jumps towards the *kochcha* of Mother Half Moon. Dusk is slowly starting to form on the earth below and Father Sun stops the celebration. The sunbeams stop the dance, pick up their drums and walk behind Father Sun towards the cloud *loklo* of rest; to prepare for the next day's celebration. Coyote looks back towards the Star Children who have stopped their fighting. And are staring dumbfounded as he gets closer to Mother Half Moon's *kochcha*.
Coyote looks back
As she wakes up
And grins like the bobcat.
The world becomes a glow with her radiating light as she walks out and kindles the fire. The embers stop dancing and look towards the direction of the wind. She smiles excitedly because she knows the goodness that is coming. The wind sweetly sings a song of joy as it blows throughout the earth and sky; the joy that is reflected within the hearts of the people. Dancing and celebration start on earth and Mother Half Moon is so filled with emotion that she grows full again. And the star children dance excitedly for this miraculous event. This is a great omen. The wind sweetly sings the song and the dance continues in the hearts of the nations of the people.

Tow<u>is</u> Hinak

'*Oye*'s fingers ran down '*Ay kooya*'s cheeks.
Cupping rainwater in his hand
He wipes away the mud; blood
That has tainted his beloved.

We Are Manik

There are things in life and they
Are manik to me.

There are things in life and they
Are like sage.

There are these things in life and they
Are cleansing.

These things,
They are manik.

They are smoke; they are purity.
They are the fire that burns.
The bush that revitalizes.

These are things in life and they are
The binding of the circle, formed by dancing feet
In one direction. These things are life. They are the symbol
Of togetherness. They are manik to me.

Paint it Blue

We are Warriors
Mighty, mighty Warriors
Fighting for our pre-ser-va-tion
Fighting for our leg-a-cy

She shouts red
Into the microphone
Her message stings like a slap
Forming a handprint
Over our mouths
Ripping out our submissive silence
Organizing to expose our reality

We are Warriors
Mighty, mighty Warriors
Fighting for our voices
Seeking out our power

Yellow drips from their lips
Oozes from their eyelids
And seduces them
With a green song.
A song, which promises renewal
While they only hear, see and speak different shades of gray.

We are Warriors
Mighty, Mighty warriors
Attacked by cowardice
We prepare for battle

She cries blue!

Honor's Song

The earth split,
rippled under 'Oyen's feet.
His feet danced back in fear
Tears fell as he felt her pain.

She moved underneath him
As he put his ear to her chest
He could hear her lifeblood being used,
Pushed,
Pumping against her.

'Oye extended his arms to comfort her
As she lay dying.
Was his power good enough here?

He needed to do something.
He needed to speak up for her.
He needed to respect her.
He needed to love her.

'Oye offered tobacco up to the ancestors
Sang a healing song as
the smell of sage purified the air,
the ancestors honored his mission.

'Oye stood up,
Blew sweet air in encouragement,
Calling the air,
Nudging him forward
Towards 'ay kooya's world.

'Oye Speaks

i.

'Oye speaks.
The ground shakes, the mountains move,
And his words fall and shatter all around him.
The world keeps changing,
he remembers that his power no longer works here.

Stomping in frustration
The earth wakes in torment.

"*Weet!*" 'Oye shouts,
Praying for clarity;
He hears a loud swoosh as a pair of black wings radiate,
descending from the sky.
Kakaali stands before 'Oye, cradling Grandmother Dreamweaver
in his arms.
They have re-entered '*ay kooya's* world.

ii.

Grandmother Dreamweaver hums a prayer song,
Patting the tule mat next to her
'*Ay kooya* sits down
A tear slides down her face.
Chachcho, my heart bleeds for our people;
my heart bleeds for the earth,
For water and for life.

Hamma, we need clarity.
We are broken.
We are sick and dying.
We need help.

Grandmother Dreamweaver nods and

continues to hum her prayer to the Ancestors.

'Oye kisses' *ay kooya* on the forehead and
Kakaali wraps her in his wings and holds her tight.

'Ay kooya, I see your pain and your fear
We are with you.

The ancestors are calling,
Honor is calling,
Hena Mi, dance the song of war

Stomp.
Dance.
Let it Rain.

Stomp.
Dance.
Let it Rain.

Let the movements of our feet
Bless you
Bless you
Let the movements of our feet
Heal you,
Let the movements of our feet
Strengthen you
Bind you
And lead you.

'Oye moves his feet in prayer.

iii.

Red handprints decorate our mouths
MUYYUM<u>TI</u>!
Is our battle cry.

Stomp!
We dance as one.
Stomp!
We sing as one.
Stomp!
We stand as one,
Stomp!
We march as one.
Stomp!
We fight as one.

Stomp!
Dance!
We are covered in blue.

The Seventh Generation is here.

Ma Talas

i.

Ma Talas
Ma 'inniiko opu talas
Ma 'inniiko opu kennetto

Ma machchaw
She shouts red into the microphone
"Stop the madness!"

Ma temma
Her message stings like a slap
"Now is our time to speak!"

Tallepuhmi! Ma temma

"Come back to your roots"
"Water them,"
"Speak with them"
And "nurture them."

Ma Talas
Ma 'inniiko opu talas
Ma 'inniiko opu kennetto

ii.

We are 'ope
'Oye says as he stands on stolen sacred ground
He remembers.

We are' ope
'Oye rips out our submissive silences
And sheds a tear
He watches.

Greed stealing our identities
Stripping us of our power,
Spreading like sickness
Bringing us to our knees.

Exposing our power hungry reality
Killing our spirits
Binding our children's souls

We are 'ope

iii.

"'U*tus*"

'O*ye* watches
The people
Congregating on stolen sacred land

"'U*tus*"

They speak.
They stand.
They stand together.

'O*ye* smiles
Listening to the blessing
He closes his eyes.

The sun rises high
In solidarity
Blanketing the earth in her warmth
Guiding the speaker's words with her comfort.

"'U'*tus*"

iv.

Their pain comes out of their lips in gusts
Their pain sings to their ancestors
Their pain rings out like the excess beat from a drum,
Stomped out like poison
Counteracting an act of being stung.
Ma machchaw
towis̲ hinak 'is "inniiko

"Win this war against colonialism."
"Braid that hair,"
"Dance around the fire,"
"Respect the water," and
"Always give love" because

We are 'ope!

Afterword

Afterword: The Voice of the Silenced

During the second half of my undergraduate career, I remember taking a Post-Colonial Literature class, which changed my view of words forever. Before this class, I had used poetry as a way to release the personal struggle I had going on inside of me. As a child, I had often felt that my voice wasn't heard and that it didn't matter to the adults who were around me. Writing became my conduit, and I was no longer silenced. For the first time I had a voice, and it felt wonderful. The first poem I wrote gave me such a rush that I wanted to continue feeling that release for as long as I could. The books I read in my Post-Colonial Lit class opened another door for me; one I didn't even knew existed. These works of fiction, non-fiction, and poetry were so powerful that they spoke to a voice that was buried deep within me. My thesis in poetry focuses on channeling the silenced and oppressed voices and brings them to light.

Finding my voice helped me understand that there is power in speaking. As I grew older, I started to see the oppression of my Native brothers and sisters and wanted to speak up for us; I wanted to defend the right for us to have a voice. Traditionally, oral histories or stories told by our elders were our voices; they were the very essence of our cultural identities. These stories provided more than just a moral compass to our children; they helped weave the fabric of who we were to become as individuals and members within our societies. The old stories share our customs and traditions with the entire community. They give a sense of purpose and respect for all who participate inside the community. Sharing old stories and weaving new ones, is in my blood. As a storyteller, it is my responsibility to continue my legacy, and give voice to our culture, through the written word.

Without having to give a full-fledged history lesson about Tribal and European / government discrimination and/or relations; I will simply say that I am a modern day California Indian who is the product of millions of Native American's whose voices have been silenced since the 1500s. I remember reading *Still I Rise* by Maya Angelou one day and the theme really stuck in my head.

> "Out of the huts of history's shame
> I rise
> Up from a past that's rooted in pain
> I rise
> I'm a black ocean, leaping and wide,
> Welling and swelling I bear in the tide.
>
> Leaving behind nights of terror and fear
> I rise
> Into a daybreak that's wondrously clear
> I rise
> Bringing the gifts that my ancestors gave,
> I am the dream and the hope of the slave.
> I rise
> I rise
> I rise (160)".

    I was a young teen when I first read this poem, but I believe that my attraction to the piece had to do with the power of her message. Even though the poem reeked of feminism, and sexual freedom, the subject matter didn't shock me because this woman was standing up for herself, something I was afraid of doing at that time in my life. Her subject matter spoke about the harsh reality of the world she lived in, the harsh reality that was ingrained in her culture. This harsh reality stemmed from the pain of the past, and a cruel present, a present she was speaking up against in hopes that it wouldn't be part of her – and her children's – future.

    Poetry itself is more than just a story. Poetry is language. It is the sounds, the nuances, and the rhythm behind the words. It is the artistic expression that challenges the very fabric of how we string words together. In her introduction to *How We Became Human*, Joy Harjo tells us her definition of what poetry is:

> "There is no separation between poetry, the stories and events that link them, or the music that holds all together, just as there is no

> separation between human, animal, plant, sky
> and earth (Harjo xxiv).

Joy Harjo is the poet that opened my eyes in my Post-Colonial Lit. Class. I was intrigued by her harsh reality – the harsh reality of all Indian peoples - that she spun together like a web of stories, stories that included the traditions, and culture of our past, with that of our present. Her poems infused the hopelessness of our current situation, brought it to light, and then gave our hope and our dreams power to prevail through this hopelessness. I wanted to know more about the situations that she spoke about within her stories. Who were these oppressed people she talked about? What made Jim drink? What made Bertha want to commit suicide? What made them feel so hopeless? And, why were they drowning in the past? These questions and their answers are the inspiration behind the characters, the stories and the worlds that I create in my poetry.

From the beginning, my poetry had a prose like form. This particular form was a rhythm in itself because it allowed me to be open with my images, and not held down by a type of structure. Like in a novel, I was able to create complex characters and a world with the freedom of a natural structure. The inhibitions and constraints of a traditional poetic form would hurt the growth of my stories and not let them breathe. The Poet David Lehman states:

> "At the juncture of imagination and body, poetry like
> dance is song is central to human   culture, in the
> mysterious fusion at the cure of mind and body."
> (Lehman xxii).

Traditional storytelling is central to our culture, like poetry it is the fabric that keeps our language, our customs, and our communities alive and even thriving. Throughout generations, these stories were spoken aloud at every ceremony, meeting, Big Time or Pow-wow. The stories were passed down and shared with every member of the community. With the creation of the written word, we storytellers, and/or poets, are able to keep this tradition alive. I recognized that if using traditional storytelling techniques worked in novels it can also work in poetry. The poem "Freedom Ride" is a perfect example of storytelling in poetic form:

> Pull the cord a stop too soon, and
> you'll find yourself walking
> a gauntlet of stares.
> Daydream, and you'll wake up
> in the stale dark of a cinema,
> Dallas playing its mistake over and over
> until even that sad reel won't stay
> stuck – there's still
> Bobby and Malcom and Memphis,
> in every corner the same
> scorched brick, darkened windows (Dove 77).

The result of crafting my poetry with traditional storytelling, made each piece stand alone, as well as build off of each other to create a new world for the readers with a list of complex characters that they would recognize. The first time I read "The Odyssey," I had no idea that a poem could be written like that. This new world of heroes, drama, culture and tradition fascinated me, and I wondered if I would ever be able to create something like this myself. During the time I read my first epic poem, I was still a beginner of poetry; writing and reading. However, the effects of the piece continued to stay with me through the course of my poetic growth where I could start writing pieces that fit the criteria of an epic poem. According to the Academy of American Poets, an epic poem consists of a long narrative verse that retells the story of a person's heroic journey. Some of the elements of these poems are superhuman deeds, adventurous, stylized language, and the blending of lyrical and dramatic traditions (poets.org).

      Storytelling is more than just words on a page, or words that dance on the tip of your tongue. A storytelling poet has a responsibility to educate her audience. Traditionally storytellers would travel from village to village creating entertaining stories that taught kids good morals, and how to act within their community. Storytelling was how we passed our traditions and culture down to the next generation. Writing as a storyteller or epic poet can be challenging at times. Storytellers are constantly coming up with new ways to captivate their audience by weaving together language, dialogue, and adventure, while teaching morals. In my opinion, every story has a hero and a villain. In our culture, the hero is known as a warrior, who is naturally on a journey to find his/her place in the community. U.S. Poet Laureate Joy Harjo says:

The poet in the role of warrior is an ancient one. The poet's road is a journey for truth, for justice. One is not liberated if another is enslaved. Compassion is the first quality of a warrior, and compassion is why we are here, why we fell from the sky. The kitchen table is the turtle's back on which this work is accomplished (Harjo xxvii).

While writing my thesis I wanted to make sure that I kept Harjo's idea of warrior in the back of my mind while playing around with language, drama, and cultural traditions in my poems, but with a modern feel. The culture and traditions of Native American people, California Indian people, have intertwined themselves with the more prominent American culture that our people have been subjected to on a daily basis. Our culture has evolved through a type of cultural adaptation where our peace-loving societies have been made into conquered, silent nations. Our nations have been suffering for centuries, and the pain shows through alcohol abuse, high suicide rates, domestic violence, extreme high school dropout rates, poverty, and loss of identity, culture and even language.

As a storyteller and a poet, it is my responsibility to be the voice of the silenced. Our culture may be suffering, but we are also rich in our blessings. When I look back at my ancestry, I see names of great warriors, chiefs, who fought to keep our ways of live alive, even if they had to do it with their lives. Heroes such as Geronimo, Crazy Horse, Red Cloud, Sitting Bull, Chief Seattle, Chief Joseph, and so many others spoke up against the injustices their people faced, and I wanted to do the same. My thesis is called 'Ope," which means *more* in my native language. It demonstrates that my Native American brothers and sisters are more than just our pain, and our loss. We are a strong, determined people. Poet Sherman Alexie, in his piece "The

Powwow at the End of the World," tells us that we need to leave our pain aside and move forward:

> I am told
> by many of you that I must forgive and so I
> shall
> after we Indians have gathered around the fire
> with that salmon
> who has three stories it must tell before sunrise:
> one story will teach us
> how to pray; another story will make us laugh
> for hours;
> the third story will give us reason to dance. I
> am told by many
> of you that I must forgive and so I shall when I
> am dancing
> with my tribe during the powwow at the end
> of the world.

Through narrative poetry, I was able to become a voice of the silenced, which helps me share our story with those who might not ever hear it.

~Yulu Ewis
Sacramento, California
August, 2020

Citations:

Alexie, Sherman. "The Powwow at the End of the World." *Poetry Foundation*, 2017, www.poetryfoundation.org/poems/47895/the-powwow-at-the-end-of-the-world.

Angelou, Maya. *The Complete Poetry Maya Angelou*. New York: Random House, 2015. Print.

Dove, Rita. *On The Bus With Rosa Parks*. New York: W.W. Norton & Company, 1999. Print.

"Epic: Poetic Form." *Academy of American Poets*, Poets.org, Feb. 21, 2014. www.m.poets.org/poetsorg/text/epic-poetic-form.

Harjo, Joy. *How We Became Human: New And Selected Poems: 1975-2001*. New York: W.W. Norton & Company, 2002. Print.

Lehman, David and Pinsky, Robert, editors. *The Best of the Best American Poetry*, 25th ed., Scribner Poetry, 2013.

Glossary

'Ache - grandchild (Southern Sierra Miwok)
'Axeki - Spirit Monster
'Ay kooya - daughter
Chachcho - Grandchild
Haws na - Prayer
Hamma - Grandmother
Helanye - Fear
Hena Mi - Rise Up
Huukuyko - Another name for Coast Miwok
Howchia - Eagle Woman
'Inniiko- People (Collective), Relatives
'Is - The
Kayaaki- Coyote-man (Southern Sierra Miwok)
Kakaali - Raven
Ka macchaw - Listen, I talk
Ka Yomu - Not a Name
Kennetto- Together
Kochcha - House
Kule - Bear
Loklo - Valley
Ma- We (more than two)
Manik - More (Southern Sierra Miwok)
Muyyumti - Love Each Other
'Olom - South, down below
'Olomko - People (Southern Pomo)
'Ope - More
'Oye - Coyote-man (Coast Miwok Creator)
Pollopaksy - Nightmare (Southern Sierra Miwok)
Talas - Stand
Tallepuhmi! - Wake Up!
Tamal Payis - Mt. Tamalpais
Temma - Matter (make a difference)
Tollepati - Free
Towis Hinak - Restore (to make a person whole)
'Unu - Mother
U'tus - Get Up

Weet! – Help! (Coast Miwok)

Color Codes:
Red – Power
Yellow – Cowardice
Green – Renewal
Gray – Detached from the world, no human emotion
Blue – Truth/Justice

Author **Yulu Ewis** is Coast Miwok and Pomo from Bay Area, California. She is a proud member of the Federated Indians of Graton Rancheria. Her work expands to that of an activist, owner of an online ghostwriting company, a freelance writer, Editor in Chief, and Co- founder of both Bear Tracks Magazine and Stop Tribal Genocide/Indigenation. The proud recipient of the Native Writer's Circle of the Americas' Library Festival: Returning the Gift's 2018 First Book Award in Poetry for 'Ope. Yulu has a Master of Science in Legal Studies and a Master of Fine Arts in Creative Writing. Yulu currently lives in Sacramento, and is the author of *DreamWeaver: A Twisted Modern Tale* , a novel. She can be reached at editor@beartracknews.com ; on Facebook under Yulu Ewis the Storyteller, Instagram under Yuluewis_author, and twitter @EwisYulu.

Artist **Tiffany Adams** (Chemehuevi/ Konkow/ Nisenan) is known for her shell work, painting, and jewelry making, Tiffany Adams is an artist, activist, and educator who incorporates her California Indian cultural practices into the fabric of her work. Tiffany's work is deeply rooted in her cultural identity as a California Indian, from her sculptures, paintings, jewelry, and basket making to her equity activism in public education, Tiffany's community-based approach to art and art making is  reflective of the ways in which identity formation is vital to artistic expression. The owner of Yellow Hammer designs based in California, Tiffany is a graduate of the Institute of American Indian Arts in Santa Fe. She is currently serving as Vice Chair of the Chemehuevi Indian Tribe of the Chemehuevi Reservation. She can be reached at *tiffanyadamsartist.com*

Carolyn M. Dunn is an Assistant Professor of Theatre and Dance at California State University Los Angeles. Dunn is a playwright, poet, muscisan, and scholar of Louisiana Creole, Tunica-Biloxi-Choctaw, and Ishak descent on her mother's side and Cherokee, Muskogee Creek/Seminole Freedmen descent on her father's. Her poetry books include *Outfoxing Coyote*; *Echolocation: Poems Indian Country, LA*; and *Stains of Burden and Dumb Luck*. Coeditor of *Through the Eye of the Deer*; *Hozho: Walking in Beauty*; and *Coyote Speaks*, her academic work has appeared in *The American Indian Culture and Research Journal*, *Belles Lettres*, and the  anthologies *American Indian Performing Arts: Critical Directions*; *Reading Native American Women*; *Cultural Representation and Contestation in Native America*, *Louisiana Creole Peoplehood: Afro-Indigeneity and Community* among others. Her plays *The Frybread Queen* premiered in Los Angeles in 2011, and *Soledad* at the Oklahoma City Native Playwright Festival in 2017. Her play Three Sisters, is set to be staged at the Tunica-Biloxi Nation Casino in Marksville, Louisiana, March 2022. She is the Managing Editor of That Painted Horse Press, which she founded alongside the late Paula Gunn Allen.